W9-ARN-404

About
Skill Builders
Grammar

by Isabelle McCoy, M.Ed.
and Leland Graham, Ph.D.

Welcome to RBP Books' Skill Builders series. Like our Summer Bridge Activities collection, the Skill Builders series is designed to make learning both fun and rewarding.

Based on NCTE (National Council of Teachers of English) standards and core curriculum, this grade 4 workbook uses a variety of fun and challenging exercises to teach and reinforce basic grammar concepts. Exercises are grade appropriate, teacher created, and classroom tested, with clear directions and examples to introduce new concepts. As students complete the exercises and games, they will learn about parts of speech, verb tense, subject-verb agreement, sentence types, capitalization, punctuation, contractions, and words such as antonyms and synonyms that often give students trouble.

A creative thinking skills section lets students have some fun with language while testing out their new knowledge.

Learning is more effective when approached with an element of fun and enthusiasm—just as most children approach life. That's why the Skill Builders combine entertaining and academically sound exercises with eye-catching graphics and fun themes—to make reviewing basic skills at school or home fun and effective, for both you and your budding scholars.

© 2003 RBP Books
All rights reserved
www.summerbridgeactivities.com

Table of Contents

Recognizing Nouns

A **noun** is a word that names a person, place, or thing.

Example:

person	Matthew
place	San Francisco
thing	bridge

Directions: Read the following sentences and circle all the nouns. (The number in parentheses indicates how many nouns are in the sentence.)

1. San Francisco, located on the coast of California, occupies a peninsula that is the southern landfall of the Golden Gate. (6)

2. Spanning the channel is the Golden Gate Bridge, a symbol of the city as the U.S. port of entry on the Pacific coast. (7)

3. The city is a popular tourist attraction, offering spectacular views from its 43 hills. (4)

4. The last three cable-car lines, now designated national historic landmarks, still cross the hills. (3)

5. To the east of Nob Hill lie Chinatown, one of the largest Chinese communities outside Asia, and Telegraph Hill, the location of the first western telegraph station. (7)

6. Fisherman's Wharf, a commercial fishing port established by 19th-century Italian immigrants, is now a row of great restaurants, souvenir shops, and hotels. (7)

7. Within San Francisco Bay is the former federal prison Alcatraz, which was considered escape-proof because of its fortresslike structure and the strong, cold currents in the surrounding waters. (6)

1

©RBP Books

Common and Proper Nouns

A **common noun** names any person, place, or thing.

Example: cat, girl, school, hippopotamus

A **proper noun** names a specific person, place, or thing and begins with a capital letter.

Example: Miss Muffet, Sally, Chicago, Sears Tower

Directions: Underline the common nouns and circle the proper nouns.

1. Lucy was surprised when her father brought home a kitten he had found while jogging in Oak Tree Park.

2. Her little sister Marie named the kitten Miss Muffet after her favorite nursery rhyme.

3. Jonathan, her older brother, drove her to Pet Town to buy food, a bowl, and a bed for Miss Muffet.

4. While they were shopping at Pet Town, Lucy saw her fourth-grade teacher, Mrs. York, buying treats for her dog, Duke.

5. When Lucy returned home, Mrs. Johnson, her mother, showed her the table leg that Miss Muffet had scratched.

6. Lucy apologized to her mother for the damage her kitten had caused and promised to train Miss Muffet.

7. Miss Muffet provided many hours of enjoyment and entertainment for the Johnson family.

8. Miss Muffet proved to be easily trained, and the family grew to love her.

©RBP Books

Forming Plural Nouns

A noun can name one or more than one person, place, or thing. A noun that names only one is called a **singular noun**. A noun that names more than one is known as a **plural noun**.

Example:

Singular	Plural
friend	friend**s**
hat	hat**s**
computer	computer**s**
skateboard	skateboard**s**

Directions: Change each singular noun to a plural noun.

Singular	Plural	Singular	Plural
1. gift		**15.** band	
2. prize		**16.** sea	
3. puddle		**17.** flag	
4. store		**18.** bird	
5. student		**19.** turkey	
6. cafeteria		**20.** key	
7. house		**21.** duck	
8. chair		**22.** boat	
9. mouth		**23.** costume	
10. paper		**24.** elephant	
11. drum		**25.** teacher	
12. floor		**26.** biscuit	
13. curtain		**27.** hamster	
14. desk		**28.** necklace	

3

Rules for Forming Plural Nouns

Most **singular nouns** can be made into **plural nouns** using one of the following rules:

1. Add -s to most nouns.	bird, bird**s**
2. If the noun ends in *y* with a consonant before the *y*, change the *y* to *i* and add -es.	penny penn**ies**
3. If the noun ends in *y* with a vowel before the *y*, just add an -s.	chimney chimney**s**
4. If the noun ends in *s*, *sh*, *ch*, or *x*, add -es.	class, class**es**
5. For some nouns ending in *f*, add -s.	chief, chief**s**
6. For some nouns ending in *f* or *fe*, change the *f* or *fe* to *v* and add -es.	wolf wol**ves**
7. Some nouns form an irregular plural.	man, **men**
8. Some nouns stay the same for singular and plural.	deer, **deer**

Directions: Change each singular noun to a plural, then using the rules listed above, identify the rule.

Singular	Plural	Rule Number
1. box		
2. coach		
3. sheep		
4. patch		
5. brush		
6. goose		
7. donkey		
8. shelf		
9. class		
10. knife		
11. mouse		
12. berry		

4

©RBP Books

Reviewing Common, Proper, and Plural Nouns

Directions: Read the following sentences and underline the common, proper, and plural nouns. Above each noun label what kind of noun it is: *C* for common, *PR* for proper, and *PL* for plural.

1. Melissa and Andrew had a beautiful baby boy named Chandler.

2. Chandler liked to drink his formula and make gurgling and cooing noises.

3. The McCoys were happy that Chandler came right before Christmas, and all of the aunts, uncles, and cousins thought he was a great baby.

4. There were more boys in the family than girls, and that made the men of the family very happy.

5. Melissa has two sisters, Andrea and Erin, and one brother, Matthew, and Andrew has two brothers, Jonathan and Richard.

6. Chandler was the first grandchild in both families, so he had many presents given to him by the family members.

7. Nana and Papa, two of the grandparents, were always taking pictures and offering to baby-sit.

© RBP Books

Collective Nouns

Nouns that group similar things, people, or animals are called **collective nouns**. A collective noun is thought of as a singular item.

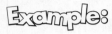 The **audience** applauded the performer.
(audience: a group of similar people)
The **herd** was grazing in the pasture.
(herd: a group of similar animals)
Give me that **bunch** of bananas!
(bunch: a group of similar things)

Directions: Underline the collective noun in each sentence.

1. A flock of geese flew north for the summer.

2. All the students in the class passed the test.

3. The committee voted for the proposal.

4. The naval fleet performed exercises for Admiral Blake.

5. Coco's litter of puppies was just adorable.

6. Oak Street's orchestra performed for the holidays.

7. The team won their final game in the championship.

8. The jury found her guilty as charged.

9. The garden club planted trees for Arbor Day.

10. A crowd gathered to hear Britney Spears perform.

www.summerbridgeactivities.com   ©RBP Books

Reviewing Nouns

Directions: Underline all nouns. Change singular nouns to plural nouns where necessary. Capitalize all proper nouns. Label the collective nouns with *CN*.

A cheetah is elegant and graceful. Running at speeds of up to 70 miles per hour, the cheetah is by far the fastest of the cat family. Cheetahs were once found in most of africa, the middle east, and india. Now they are found mostly in sub-Saharan Africa. The cheetah has long, muscular leg; a small, round head; a long neck; and special pad on its foot for traction. Even though the cheetah is fast, it cannot speed for long distance because it may overheat.

When a cheetah makes a kill, it eats quickly and keeps an eye out for scavenger, such as leopards and vulture. They usually hunt smaller antelopes and impalas.

If hunting together, they may seek out a herd of zebras or wildebeests. Even though the cheetah is fast, it depends on cover to hide in as it stalks its prey. The cheetah gets as close as possible to its prey and then uses a burst of speed to outrun its quarry.

© RBP Books

Introducing Pronouns

A **pronoun** is a word that takes the place of a noun.

Singular Pronouns		Plural Pronouns	
I	me	we	us
you		you	
she	her	they	them
he	him	they	them
it		they	them

Directions: Underline the pronouns in each sentence.

1. Jennifer and I wanted to go to the store.

2. While we were at the store, we bought the groceries for next week.

3. Jennifer wanted to buy some meat, potatoes, and vegetables, and she used a check to pay for them.

4. I wanted her to help me pick out some food for a special dinner.

5. It was going to be a surprise dinner party for our mother and father.

6. They were having an anniversary, and we wanted it to be very special.

7. It would take us all day to clean the house and cook the food for them.

8. She and I had a great time working together for the party.

www.summerbridgeactivities.com ©RBP Books

Introducing Pronouns

Directions: Circle the pronouns that can be used for each noun.

Nouns	Pronouns	Pronouns	Pronouns
1. Mary	she	he	her
2. Juan	it	him	he
3. tools	them	it	they
4. doll	her	them	it
5. Seattle	he	it	she
6. sister	you	she	her
7. friends	they	them	it
8. computer	it	he	her
9. Dr. Chen	she	he	her
10. flowers	him	they	them

Directions: Choose the pronoun that could be used to replace the underlined word(s).

11. <u>Jason</u> wanted to go to the music store alone. (Him, He)

12. The dog was running to get the <u>soup bone</u>. (they, it)

13. Many people feel happy when <u>children</u> sing. (they, them)

14. <u>Mom, Dad, and Mary</u> often eat together. (Them, They)

15. <u>Tanisha</u> used the home computer each day. (Her, She)

16. <u>Isabelle</u>, take this newspaper to Mr. Scott. (You, They)

17. <u>Jennifer and I</u> bought a party gift for Dottie. (Them, We)

18. <u>Rover</u> ran after the ball when it was thrown. (He, Him)

© RBP Books

Subject Pronouns

A pronoun can be used as a subject of a sentence. The subject tells whom or what the sentence concerns. Not all pronouns can be used as subjects. Only the **subject pronouns** listed below can be used as the subjects of sentences.

Subject Pronouns

Singular	Plural
I	we
you	you
he, she, it	they

Directions: Choose the correct subject pronoun listed above to take the place of the underlined word or words in each sentence.

1. <u>Dr. Smith</u> traveled to Nigeria to study the hippopotamuses.

2. <u>The hippos</u> spend most of the day in the water.

3. When <u>a hippo</u> sinks underwater, its nose and ears close.

4. <u>The mother hippo</u> protects the babies from danger.

5. When <u>a hippo male in the group</u> challenges another, he opens his mouth to reveal his long canine teeth.

6. <u>A hippo</u> is an excellent swimmer and can hold its breath for about five minutes.

7. <u>Hippos</u> fight violently and often wound or kill one another.

www.summerbridgeactivities.com ©RBP Books

Object Pronouns

Object pronouns (*me, you, him, her, it, us,* and *them*) may be used after action verbs or after prepositions.

Example: The young girl thanked **me**. (*Me* is an object pronoun after an action verb.)

I went to the zoo with **him**. (*Him* is an object pronoun after a preposition.)

Delores asked **them** to explain how to create a Web site on a computer. (*Them* is an object pronoun after an action verb.)

Directions: In the following sentences, the subject pronoun is listed to the left of the sentence. Write the object pronoun in the blank provided.

they   **1.** The guide showed _____ how to make fudge.

I   **2.** Please give the present to _____.

we   **3.** The school provided _____ with our supplies.

he   **4.** Lucy took a picture of _____.

it   **5.** The baby really wanted _____.

you   **6.** Gary wanted to give _____ a picture of Lucy.

she   **7.** Mary tapped John and asked if he would give _____ a valentine.

we   **8.** The present was from both of _____.

they   **9.** Thomas and Martha wanted to travel to Mexico with _____.

© RBP Books

Reviewing Subject and Object Pronouns

Directions: Underline the correct pronoun. Write the pronoun in the chart at the bottom; then tell if it is a subject or an object pronoun.

1. (I, Me) wanted to travel to Italy for a vacation.

2. My friend Juanita wanted to go with (I, me).

3. (We, Us) traveled by plane to Rome, the capital city of Italy.

4. In Rome (she, her) favorite site was the Colosseum.

5. While in Rome, (they, them) visited the Sistine Chapel where Michelangelo, a well-known painter and sculptor, painted the ceiling of the chapel.

6. (His, Him) paintings can be found in many museums around the world.

7. Next, (we, us) visited the Leaning Tower of Pisa.

8. When I returned from Italy, I wrote a story about (he, it).

Pronoun	Subject or Object
1.	
2.	
3.	
4.	
5.	
6.	
7.	
8.	

©RBP Books

Possessive Pronouns

A **possessive pronoun** is a pronoun that shows ownership (*my, his, her, its, their, our,* and *your*). These possessive pronouns come before nouns. Unlike a possessive noun, a possessive pronoun does not use an apostrophe.

Example: The face of the Sphinx is 13 feet wide, and **its** eyes are 6 feet high.

Workers who created the Sphinx gave it **their** king's face.

Directions: Read the following paragraphs and underline the possessive pronouns.

Jason, Mary, Tina, and I wanted to visit Egypt. Our trip to Egypt would not be complete without a visit to the Great Sphinx. After seeing the amazing monument, Jason said that his impression of the Sphinx would last for decades. Mary and Tina wanted their pictures taken as they sat on camels in front of the Sphinx. My other friends could not believe that we were actually visiting such an ancient site until they saw our photographs.

The Great Sphinx was created over 4,500 years ago and was buried for most of its life. Some experts say it was built after the pyramid of Chephren was completed. It may have been built to guard his tomb. The statue is crumbling today because of wind, humidity, and smog. Scientists are trying to restore it, but their efforts have not been successful thus far.

13

© RBP Books

Possessive Pronouns

Possessive pronouns show ownership. The following possessive pronouns can stand alone: *mine*, *yours*, *hers*, *his*, *ours*, and *theirs*.

Example: That red and blue toy train is **mine**.
The dog we found is now **yours**.

Directions: Circle the possessive pronoun that can be used in the blank.

1. Maria thought it was _____ to give (she, hers, our).

2. Is that green car _____ (my, our, yours)?

3. The dog was _____ before it was Tim's (mine, she, he).

4. Which one of these coats is _____ (his, I, you)?

5. The Sheltie puppy was _____ (my, theirs, her).

6. This house is not yours; it is _____ (he, she, ours).

7. You read your story; now I will read _____ (mine, I, me).

8. This television is now _____ (they, them, theirs).

9. Antwon wanted _____ video game returned (he, his, him).

10. We introduced Carlos to another friend of _____ (your, ours, their).

11. The *Spirit of St. Louis* was the name of _____ airplane. (his, he, him)

12. Why doesn't Maria come to my house as often as she comes to _____ (you, yours, her)?

©RBP Books

Contractions with Pronouns

A **contraction** is the combined form of two words. Some contractions are formed by combining a pronoun and a verb. Use an apostrophe (') to replace the letter or letters that are omitted. Study this chart of contractions formed from pronouns.

Pronoun and Verb	Contraction
I have	I've
he has	he's
she has	she's
it has	it's
you have	you've
we have	we've
they have	they've
I had	I'd
you had	you'd
he had	he'd
we had	we'd
I am	I'm
he is	he's
she is	she's
it is	it's
you are	you're
we are	we're
they are	they're
I will	I'll
you will	you'll
she will	she'll
they will	they'll

Directions: What contractions are formed from the following pairs of words?

1. they will   **2.** you have   **3.** I will

_____   _____   _____

15

Working with Contractions
Formed from Pronouns

Directions: Write the two words for each underlined contraction.

Example: I've purchased a new computer. **I have**

1. <u>I'm</u> going to take a computer class to learn how to create a Web site.

2. <u>You're</u> never going to believe what I have learned after these few classes.

3. <u>They're</u> taking a computer class to learn how to use the Internet.

4. <u>You'd</u> better purchase a computer so that we can email each other.

5. <u>I've</u> received 14 emails since Tuesday.

6. Maurice said that <u>he's</u> very happy with his new flat-screen monitor.

7. <u>It's</u> certainly easier to communicate with my friends now that I have a computer.

8. <u>We'd</u> never have believed that we would see our father using a computer.

9. Now <u>he's</u> become a computer whiz!

10. <u>We're</u> sure that your parents would enjoy using a computer also.

16

©RBP Books

Reviewing Pronouns

Directions: Replace the underlined noun(s) with a pronoun.

1. Ali said, "Jeffrey will drive <u>Jeffrey's</u> car to the shop."

2. <u>Marvin and Thelia</u> were interested in learning more about photography.

3. <u>Frieda</u> answered the phone, hoping it was Christine calling.

4. Where did <u>Ninoska and Helena</u> find those beautiful potted plants?

Directions: Underline the possessive pronouns.

5. Her raincoat kept her dry during the storm.

6. Harold gave the children rides on his horse.

7. She will buy the puppy its doghouse.

8. Their mother worried about the children's safety.

Directions: Write proper nouns to replace the underlined subject and object pronouns.

9. <u>Their</u> friends enjoyed listening to her play the piano.

10. Mother asked my sister and <u>me</u> to finish our chores.

11. <u>She</u> wanted the doctor to cure the flu.

Directions: Replace each contraction with a pronoun and a verb.

12. they're   **13.** she'd   **14.** you'll

© RBP Books

Recognizing Action Verbs

A **verb** is a word that can show action. A verb tells what a person or thing is doing.

Example: My brother **rides** his new bicycle.

Sunflowers **grow** very tall in the summer.

Directions: Circle the verb(s) in the following sentences. (The number in parentheses indicates how many verbs are in the sentence.)

1. Tornadoes form from thunderstorms when cold and warm air meet. (2)

2. Winds in a tornado often reach more than 320 miles per hour. (1)

3. If you live in a house with a basement, go to it immediately. (2)

4. Flying objects in a tornado cause the most deaths. (1)

5. Tornadoes break tree branches and damage houses. (2)

Directions: Complete each sentence with a verb from the Word Bank.

Word Bank

move	lie	indicates
announced	protect	form

6. _____ yourself when tornado warnings are issued.

7. Tornadoes _____ in many states and countries.

8. Tornadoes usually _____ from southwest to northeast.

9. If you are outside, _____ in a ditch or low-lying area.

10. A tornado warning is _____ when a tornado has been spotted.

11. A tornado watch _____ conditions are favorable for a tornado to form.

18

© RBP Books

Linking Verbs

A **linking verb** does not show action. Instead of showing action, it links the subject to the rest of the sentence. Forms of the verb *to be* are common linking verbs.

Singular	**Plural**
(I) am	(we) are
(you) are	(you) are
(she, he, it) is	(they) are

 **Example:** I **am** nine years old.
We **are** on the Redbirds baseball team.

Directions: Underline the linking verb in each sentence.

1. Minneapolis is a large city in Minnesota.

2. Where were you during the tornado last week?

3. Arlene and Darlene Anderson are identical twins.

4. We were in Colorado Springs when our car broke down.

5. I am on my way to purchase a new CD burner.

6. Nahom was an excellent violinist in the orchestra.

7. Stephanie and I were on our way to try out for the softball team.

8. Roberto and Ricardo are both in the rodeo competition this summer.

9. The best pitcher on our baseball team is Arkelius.

© RBP Books   Grammar Grade 4—RBP0113

Verb Tenses

In addition to showing action or linking subjects to the rest of the sentence, verbs indicate time. This time is called **tense**. There are three tenses: **present**, **past**, and **future**.

Present tense verbs show action that is happening now.

Example: I **sing** in the church choir. (action verb)

Melvin **is** in the church choir. (linking verb)

Past tense verbs show action that happened earlier.

Example: Lois **sang** in the church choir.

Ariel **was** in the church choir.

Future tense verbs show action that will happen in the future.

Example: Arnita **will sing** in the church choir.

I **shall sing** in the church choir today.

Directions: Write the verbs below using the tenses shown.

Tense	walk	ride	talk
1. Present			
2. Past			
3. Future			

Directions: Choose the correct word; change its tense if needed.

walk   go   operate

use   build   gather

4. Jacob _____ to the theater this evening.

5. Squirrels _____ acorns and nuts for the winter.

6. As I _____ through the snow, I saw many snowmen.

7. The doctor _____ on my mother tomorrow morning.

8. He _____ all of the hot water when he took his shower.

9. Beavers _____ dams in the river every year.

20

© RBP Books

Reviewing Verb Tenses

Directions: Underline the verb(s) in each sentence. Write the tense(s) on the line below the sentence.

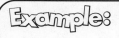 Jonathan **played** baseball last summer.
past tense

1. Andre will play first base in tomorrow's game.

   _____

2. The score in yesterday's game was five to two.

   _____

3. Maria is playing in the outfield for the Northlake Bears.

   _____

4. The pitcher threw three straight fastballs.

   _____

5. Will the Park Raiders be able to defeat the champions?

   _____

6. The third baseman made a double play.

   _____

7. Coach Williams assisted the catcher with her equipment.

   _____

8. The umpire shouted, "You're out, buddy!"

   _____

9. The batter is standing in the box ready to swing.

   _____

© RBP Books

Identifying Helping Verbs

Helping verbs are sometimes used with action verbs. The following is a list of commonly used helping verbs:

am	has	can	might
is	have	may	must
are	had	should	do
were	shall	would	did
was	will	could	does

Example: James Naismith <u>was</u> <u>born</u> on November 6, 1861.

Directions: Complete each sentence using a helping verb from the list above.

1. Mr. Naismith _____ create the game of basketball.

2. In 1894, James _____ married to Maude Shermann.

3. Basketball _____ played on an indoor court.

4. I ___ going to practice with my team, the Blue Devils.

5. You _____ go with me to pick up my basketball uniform.

6. My coach _____ like for you to join our team.

7. Henrietta _____ have gone to the store before practice.

8. Frank _____ play most any position on the team.

9. If James Naismith _____ alive today, he would be proud.

22

© RBP Books

Helping Verbs

A **verb phrase** is made of a main verb and one or more helping verbs.

Example: The swimming instructor **is giving** lessons today.
is = helping verb, **giving** = main verb

Directions: In the following sentences, underline the helping verb(s) and circle the main verb.

1. Melvin has learned the backstroke this summer.

2. Have you ever gone to Town Lake to swim?

3. Iris and Helen are practicing for the swim meet.

4. The final competition will be held at Lake Arrowhead.

5. The swimming coach was driving the team to the meet.

6. Did you go to the swimming meet to watch your sister?

7. I am competing in the 4 x 100 relay race at Lake Arrowhead.

8. Chuck is swimming faster each day.

9. Ted Turner should win the final swimming competition.

10. Valerie was excited to win her first swimming medal.

23

Irregular Verbs

Verbs that do not add -ed to form the past tense are called **irregular verbs**. The spelling of these verbs changes.

Present	Past
swim, swims	swam
run, runs	ran
take, takes	took

Directions: Write the past tense of each verb in parentheses.

1. Teiko _____ (do) his best to eat all the food on his plate.

2. Did you see how the quarterback _____ (run) for a touchdown?

3. Michael _____ (take) a long walk in Medlock Park along the riverfront.

4. After breakfast, Thomas _____ (go) to ride his new red bicycle around the block

5. The new puppy _____ (sleep) all night long.

6. Martha _____ (begin) each day with meditation.

7. The little boy has _____ (wore) a hole in his socks.

8. The airplane _____ (fly) from Miami to New York.

9. The team _____ (win) their fourth straight game tonight.

10. How could she have _____ (sell) so many boxes of cookies in one week?

 ©RBP Books

Subject-Verb Agreement

A verb in the present tense must **agree** with the subject of the sentence. In other words, the subject and verb must work together. If the subject is singular, add -*s* to the verb; if plural, do not add an ending to the verb.

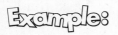 A computer **works** faster than a typewriter.
(singular subject—add -*s* to the verb)
Computers **work** faster than typewriters.
(plural subject—no ending to the verb)

Directions: Choose the verb that correctly completes the sentence.

1. A thunderstorm (cause, causes) problems with traffic.

2. Puddles (form, forms) after the rain has ended.

3. Lightning (strike, strikes) during a thunderstorm.

4. The damage from the storm (create, creates) problems for the power company.

5. During a drought, people (cheer, cheers) the news of a coming thunderstorm.

6. The puppy (cry, cries) when it hears the thunder.

7. Floods (occur, occurs) often in our area after a bad thunderstorm.

8. Many accidents (happen, happens) during rush hour traffic when there is a thunderstorm.

9. Can't thunderstorms (ruin, ruins) a picnic?

© RBP Books

Reviewing Verbs

Directions: Study the list of words below. Circle only the verbs.

move	walk	ruin	Turner
elephant	sang	run	shall
swimming	game	Melvin	rides
James	learned	flying	basketball
practice	coach	Minnesota	may
computer	breakfast	indicate	did
instructor	went	visit	cry
protect	fly	were	strike
are	sold	am	lake
should	cause	must	take

Directions: Write your own sentences about skating using the following verbs. Feel free to change the tense of the verb.

1. fall

_____

2. race

_____

3. skate

_____

4. challenge

_____

5. compete

_____

6. enjoy

_____

www.summerbridgeactivities.com

© RBP Books

Noun and Verb Review

Directions: Read the following pairs of sentences. Decide if the underlined word is a noun or a verb. Next, write *noun* or *verb* on the line provided.

> **Example:** Mother is cooking <u>duck</u> for dinner. **noun**
>
> When you enter the tree house, make sure you <u>duck</u>. **verb**

1. The bride proudly wore her wedding <u>ring</u>. _____

<u>Ring</u> the bell to announce dinner. _____

2. Please <u>dress</u> yourself properly before coming to dinner. _____

Yvette wore her blue <u>dress</u> to church. _____

3. <u>Cook</u> the turkey until it is well done. _____

The <u>cook</u> enjoyed preparing meals. _____

4. Can you <u>paint</u> this landscape scene? _____

I prefer green <u>paint</u> for my bedroom. _____

5. Have you seen my right <u>skate</u>? _____

I can <u>skate</u> better than Dorothy. _____

6. The dolphin was swimming in the <u>wave</u>. _____

<u>Wave</u> good bye to your grandparents! _____

© RBP Books

Nouns, Pronouns, and Verbs Crossword

Directions: Use the clues below to complete the crossword puzzle on nouns, pronouns, and verbs.

Across

3. a pronoun used as the object of a sentence
4. a type of noun that names a specific person, place, or thing
6. type of verb that links the subject with the rest of the sentence
9. a word that names a person, place, or thing
10. a pronoun that shows ownership
11. nouns that group certain people, things, or animals

Down

1. a type of noun that names any person, place, or thing
2. type of verb used with action verbs
5. a word that takes the place of a noun
7. verbs that change their spelling to form the past tense
8. a pronoun used as the subject of a sentence
12. a word that shows action

28

©RBP Books

Introducing Adjectives

An **adjective** is a word that describes a noun or pronoun. It tells **what kind** (big, blue, high), **how many** (one, all, few), or **which one** (each, any, that).

Example: Soccer is the most **popular** sport in Mexico. (what kind)

Mexico has **six** main land regions. (how many)

This river, the Rio Grande, is north of Mexico. (which one)

Directions: Underline the adjectives; then write above the adjectives *what kind, how many,* or *which one.*

1. Lake Chapala is Mexico's largest lake.

2. Many people live in Mexico City, the capital.

3. Those tortillas are made with corn flour and taste delicious.

4. One holiday that is popular is Cinco de Mayo.

5. Nine days before Christmas, Mexicans celebrate by reenacting Mary and Joseph's searching for a room at the inn.

6. These nine ceremonies are called *posadas.*

7. Orizaba is Mexico's highest point above sea level.

8. Tenochtitlán is the ancient Aztec capital.

9. Diego Rivera painted those beautiful Mexican murals.

© RBP Books

Adjectives: Using *A*, *An*, and *The*

There are some special adjectives called **articles**—*a*, *an*, and *the*.

With singular nouns
 Use *a* before words that begin with a consonant sound.
 Use *an* before words that begin with a vowel sound or
  a silent *h*.
 Use *the* if the noun names a particular person, place, or
  thing.
With plural nouns
 Use *the* before a plural noun.

 **A** hippopotamus cooled himself in **the** river.
An elephant gave himself **a** mud bath.
The zebras protected their young from **the** lions.

Directions: Complete the paragraph below using the articles *a*, *an*, and *the*.

____ African parrot lives in tropical areas. One variety is ____ rose-ringed parakeet. It has ____ long tail, ____ bright red bill, and ____ bright green head. ____ nine species of lovebirds are ____ only small African parrots. ____ lovebirds have short, rounded tails and rather large bills. ____ lovebirds got their name because they were thought to mate for life. ____ large, gray parrot from ____ West African rain forest is ____ popular pet because it can learn to say words.

©RBP Books

Recognizing Adjectives

All of these adjectives can be used to describe turtles: *green*, *slow*, *cold-blooded*, *many*, *young*, and *freshwater*.

Directions: Place a check mark in front of any adjective that would correctly complete the sentence. Then finish the sentences below.

1. ____ greatly
____ the
____ species
____ largest

_____ turtle is the leatherback.

2. ____ the
____ some
____ kinds

_____ turtles, like ____ sea turtles, can't hide in their shells.

3. ____ one
____ fastest
____ lived
____ the

_____ of _____ turtles is the sea turtle.

4. ____ brown
____ green
____ some
____ black

_____ turtles have _____, _____, or _____ shells.

Directions: Place a check mark in front of any adjective that would correctly complete the sentence. Then finish the sentences below.

5. A few turtles have bright green, orange, red, or yellow markings.

6. The head of most turtles is covered by hard scales.

7. Land turtles have heavy, short, clublike legs and feet.

8. Most freshwater turtles hibernate by burrowing into the warm, muddy bottom of a pond or other body of water.

© RBP Books

Using Predicate Adjectives

An adjective can come after the word it describes. It usually follows a form of the verb *be* (*am*, *is*, *are*, *was*, and *were*) and is called a **predicate adjective**.

Example: The clown **was** <u>short</u>, <u>fat</u>, and <u>funny</u>.
John, the lion tamer, **is** <u>brave</u> and <u>daring</u>.

Directions: Underline the predicate adjectives in the following sentences.

1. She was rather angry until she heard that her parents had purchased circus tickets.
2. Anna was happy and excited about going to the circus.
3. Anna's parents were kind enough to buy popcorn and soft drinks.
4. The smell of circus animals was powerful and overwhelming.
5. Once the circus started, the performers were colorful, talented, and entertaining.
6. Suddenly, out of nowhere, appeared a clown who was tall and funny.
7. The lions and tigers were loud, fierce, and scary.
8. Many trapeze artists performed and were graceful and daring.
9. Her favorite act, the wonderful dancing bears, was lively and hilarious.

www.summerbridgeactivities.com   © RBP Books

Adjective Comparisons

When adjectives are used to compare people, places, or things, there are certain spelling rules to follow.

1. For most adjectives, add -*er* or -*est* to the end.

   kind   kind**er**   kind**est**

2. For adjectives ending with a consonant preceded by a single vowel, double the final consonant and add -*er* or -*est*.

   hot   hot**ter**   hot**test**

3. For adjectives that end in an *e*, drop the *e* and add -*er* or -*est*.

   close   clos**er**   clos**est**

4. For adjectives that end in a *y* preceded by a consonant, change the *y* to *i* and add -*er* or -*est*.

   noisy   nois**ier**   nois**iest**

Directions: Complete the following chart using the rules listed above.

Adjective	Add -*er*	Add -*est*
1. old		
2. clear		
3. tall		
4. quick		
5. fast		
6. strong		
7. dry		
8. thin		
9. red		
10. long		
11. happy		
12. cute		
13. tiny		
14. loud		
15. angry		

© RBP Books

Comparative and Superlative Adjectives

To compare two nouns, use the **comparative** form of the adjective. The comparative form is made by adding -er to most adjectives. When an adjective contains three or more syllables, however, use the word *more* before the adjective instead of adding -er.

To compare three or more nouns, use the **superlative** form of the adjective. The superlative form is made by adding -est to most adjectives. When an adjective contains three or more syllables, however, use the word *most* before the adjective instead of adding -est.

Directions: Write the correct form of the adjective in parentheses to complete each sentence.

Example: New Orleans is <u>larger</u> than Macon. (large)

Many people consider New Orleans America's <u>most interesting</u> city. (interest)

1. New Orleans is the _____ city in Louisiana.   (big)

2. It is also one of the world's _____ ports.   (busy)

3. New Orleans is _____ than Boulder, Colorado.   (old)

4. Several of New Orleans's _____ _____ structures border Jackson Square.   (historic)

5. The _____ levees lie along the Mississippi River and Lake Pontchartrain.   (long)

6. City Park in New Orleans is one of the nation's _____ city-owned parks.   (large)

7. Atlanta is _____ east than New Orleans.   (far)

8. The Pontalba Buildings are the city's _____ _____ residences.   (fashionable)

© RBP Books

Special Adjectives

When you use the special adjectives *good* and *bad* to compare, you need to change their forms. Change *good* to *better* when comparing two things. Change *good* to *best* when comparing three or more things.

Example: The student gave a **good** answer.

John's answer was **better** than the other student's.

Change the adjective *bad* to *worse* when comparing two things. Change *bad* to *worst* when comparing three or more things.

Example: The burned liver tasted **worse** than last time.

The beets were the **worst** I have ever eaten.

Directions: Write the correct form of the adjective in parentheses.

1. The _____ dessert I have ever eaten was a hot fudge sundae.   (good)

2. That spinach casserole was the _____ vegetable I have ever tasted.   (bad)

3. We grilled sirloin steaks that were _____ than any other we have ever cooked.   (good)

4. Chef Carlos is _____ than Chef Pierre at baking cakes.   (good)

5. The canned spaghetti I ate today was _____ than Mother's home-cooked spaghetti.   (bad)

6. Jeffrey is a _____ chef than Mary Ann.   (good)

© RBP Books

Reviewing Adjectives

Directions: Two sentences using adjectives are given below. Write the letter of the correctly written sentence in the blank.

1. a. Lake Lanier is Georgia's largest lake.
   b. Lake Lanier is Georgia's larger lake.

2. a. The most hotter day of the year is today.
   b. The hottest day of the year is today.

3. a. Mrs. Potter is the worstest teacher I've ever had.
   b. Mrs. Potter is the worst teacher I've ever had.

4. a. This is the best recipe for pecan brownies.
   b. This is the most best recipe for pecan brownies.

5. a. The harder class I've ever taken is geography.
   b. The hardest class I've ever taken is geography.

6. a. An new refrigerator is extremely expensive.
   b. A new refrigerator is extremely expensive.

7. a. An oak tree is stronger than a pine tree.
   b. A oak tree is strongest than a pine tree.

8. a. Our spring concert was bestest than the first one.
   b. Our spring concert was better than the first one.

9. a. Those flowers are more beautiful than these.
   b. Those flowers are more beautifuler than these.

36

© RBP Books

Introducing Adverbs

An **adverb** is a word that describes or tells more about the action of a verb. Adverbs answer the questions **how, when, where,** or **to what extent**.

Example: Hawaiian crafts are **carefully** preserved.   (how)
Hawaiian history was oral **before** it was written.   (when)
Kilauea Volcano is **there** on the island.   (where)
Polynesians traveled **miles** to arrive at these islands.   (to what extent)

Directions: Underline the adverbs in the following sentences:

1. Hawaii's King Kamehameha ruled his people fairly.

2. Once the islands of Hawaii were barren.

3. Now tropical plants grow quickly in Hawaii's climate.

4. Early settlers thoughtfully brought many species of plants and animals to the islands.

5. Hula competitions are held formally each year.

6. One hundred thirty-two volcanic peaks emerge gracefully from the Pacific Ocean, making up the Hawaiian Islands.

7. Surprisingly, Hawaii is the only state to have a throne room.

8. Many years ago, feathered garments were worn only by men of high birth.

9. Yellow feathers were scarcest and thus most prized.

©RBP Books

Practicing with Adverbs

Many adverbs end in *-ly: quickly, slowly, secretly, carefully*. However, some common adverbs do not end in *-ly: never, not, almost, very, now, often*.

Directions: Underline each adverb. Draw an arrow to the verb it describes.

Example: The Scott family <u>suddenly</u> decided to move to Rhode Island.
(*Suddenly* is an adverb that describes the verb *decided*.)

1. The Hercules Moving Company arrived early to begin the packing.

2. Mr. Scott has already left for Rhode Island.

3. The children watched forlornly as their toys were packed.

4. Mrs. Scott watched as the movers carefully packed the dishes.

5. John, one of the movers, tried walking backwards with some boxes but fell.

6. Fortunately, none of the items in the boxes were broken.

7. The movers had difficulty loading the Scotts' piano.

8. Because of the threat of rain, the movers quickly loaded the rest of the boxes.

9. Soon the Scott family would have to say good-bye to their neighbors.

10. Completely packed, the moving van left early on Friday.

©RBP Books

Recognizing Adverbs

Using your imagination, complete the following story with adverbs. Remember: Adverbs tell when, where, how, or to what extent.

"Julie's Trip to Space Camp"

Julie was _____ excited about going to the Florida Space Camp. Her parents had _____ surprised her with tickets for this trip. One of Julie's friends, Rose, _____ decided to join her. Together they would _____ travel to Florida.

When they arrived at space camp, they _____ found their rooms and met their guides. _____ the trainees and their teammates were divided into two crews: the mission control crew and the flight crew. _____, the mission control team was _____ trained on computer and communication operating systems. The flight crew was _____ trained on operating the Orbiter. Some members of the flight crew were trained as mission specialists. The mission specialists _____ learned about space suits and took a walk in space. The mission control crew kept everything going _____. As the mission wrapped up, the crew cheered and applauded _____.

Julie and Rose _____ enjoyed their adventure at space camp in Florida this summer.

© RBP Books

Comparative Adverbs

Most adverbs, like adjectives, can show comparison. When an adverb compares two actions, add *-er*; if the adverb ends in *-ly* or is *more* than one syllable, add *more* in front of it. When adverbs compare three or more actions, add *-est*; if the adverb ends in *-ly* or is more than one syllable, add *most* in front of it.

Example:

> Adverb with one action:
> Jennifer walks **quickly**.
>
> Adverb comparing two actions:
> Jennifer walks **quicker** than Melissa.
>
> Adverb comparing three or more actions:
> Jennifer walks **quickest** of all.

Directions: Finish the following sentences with a comparative form of the underlined adverb. You may need to add **more** or **most** to show comparison.

1. Muriel drove <u>fast</u> in the race.
   Muriel drove _____ than Jonathan.
   Donald drove the _____ of all.

2. Martha danced <u>gracefully</u> at the recital.
   Martha danced _____ _____ than Susan.
   Stephanie danced _____ _____ of all.

3. Fernando jumps <u>high</u>.
   Fernando jumps _____ than Mark.
   Isabelle jumps _____ of all the children.

4. Coach Muir blew her whistle <u>loudly</u>.
   Coach Muir blew her whistle _____ _____ than Sam.
   Mr. Freed blew his whistle _____ _____ of everyone.

www.summerbridgeactivities.com

© RBP Books

Misused Adverbs

Good, *bad*, *real*, and *sure* are adjectives that describe nouns or pronouns. *Well*, *surely*, *really*, and *badly* are adverbs that describe verbs.

Adjectives	Adverbs
Good is an adjective when it describes a noun.	*Good* is never used as an adverb.
Well is an adjective when it refers to good or poor health.	*Well* is an adverb when it is used to tell that something is done capably or effectively.
Bad is an adjective when it describes a noun.	*Badly* is an adverb that describes a verb.
Real is an adjective that means true or genuine.	*Really* is an adverb that describes a verb.
Sure is an adjective when it describes a noun.	*Surely* is an adverb that describes a verb.

Directions: Select the correct word to complete the sentence.

1. Henry plays basketball (good, well).
2. Perry Mason (sure, surely) solved the murder case.
3. Zelda (real, really) wants to bake those brownies.
4. Everyone in class listens (good, well) to the directions.
5. Our team lost (bad, badly) at the state finals.
6. Richard behaved (bad, badly) on the field trip.
7. How long did it take to decide who (real, really) stole it?
8. Susie (sure, surely) will receive an A on her art project.
9. Agatha describes her family (good, well).
10. (Sure, Surely) the teacher will not give us a test today.

© RBP Books

Double Negatives

When writing sentences, you may use the word *no* or words that mean *no*. A word that makes a sentence mean *no* is a negative. The words *no, nobody, no one, nothing, none, nowhere*, and *never* are **negatives**. The word *not* and contractions made with not are also negatives. Never use two negatives together in a sentence.

Correct	**Incorrect**
No one ever told me that my hair was too long.	**No one never** told me that my hair was too long.
There were **none** of those books left on the shelf.	There **weren't none** of those books left on the shelf.

Directions: Which word in the parentheses is correct?

1. Beverly wasn't (ever, never) going to believe her brother.

2. Clint couldn't go (nowhere, anywhere) until he finished his chores.

3. Fortunately, I was sure (no one, anyone) was hiding in the closet.

4. Poetry was (never, ever) very interesting to Donald.

5. He wanted (anything, nothing) from the grocery store.

6. I called, but (nobody, anybody) was home today.

7. Isn't (anyone, no one) going to Mary's birthday party?

8. There won't be (no, any) cake left after the party.

42

©RBP Books

Reviewing Adverbs

Directions: Underline all the adverbs in each sentence.

1. Maurice sang very beautifully in the chorus.
2. The rabbit hopped quickly and quietly across the yard.
3. Complete your homework carefully and accurately.
4. Who finished faster, you or your brother George?
5. Sarah politely introduced her mother to her teacher.
6. Can't you get dressed faster than Matt?
7. The play was extremely long and very boring.
8. David recently visited Spain and Morocco.
9. Sherrie can do her work more skillfully than Karen.
10. The revised manuscript will arrive today.

Directions: Underline the correct adverb in the parentheses.

11. Which of these teams played (worse, worst)?
12. The quarterback ran (faster, fastest) than Ronnie.
13. The big dog barked (loud, loudly) all night long.
14. Mother will (sure, surely) receive a raise this month.
15. The photographer worked (good, well) under pressure.
16. Of all the violinists, Lee performed (badliest, most badly).
17. The guests (unexpected, unexpectedly) arrived early.
18. The teenager walked (clumsily, clumsier) into the room.
19. The fourth-grade class worked (steadily, most steadily) for an hour.
20. Leaves were scattered (nowhere, everywhere).

Directions: Use the following adverbs and create your own sentences.

21. recently
22. soon
23. more often
24. badly
25. most easily

43

© RBP Books

Introducing Prepositions

A **preposition** is a word placed before a noun or pronoun to show its relationship to another word in the sentence. A **prepositional phrase** is a group of words that begins with a preposition and ends with the object of the preposition. Some commonly used prepositions are as follows:

below	about	between	under
beside	from	behind	near
above	through	inside	down
in	after	toward	off
to	except	around	at
during	on	upon	with

Example: The bird flew **through** the fluffy clouds.
The squirrels run **up** the old oak tree.

Directions: Underline the prepositional phrases in each of the sentences.

1. Paul and Fran raced over the rolling hills in the morning.

2. The birds built a nest of pine straw and twigs in the trees.

3. The bird feeder was located above the white fence.

4. The car came barreling around the corner of the street.

5. I found a small, tan puppy sitting on the porch steps.

6. The prizes were divided between Travis and me.

7. Everyone except Harry ran in this morning's race.

©RBP Books

Using Prepositions

Directions: In the following sentences, circle the preposition and underline the object of the preposition. Remember: The object of a preposition can be a noun or a pronoun.

> **Example:** Terrence sang (with) the <u>choir</u>.
>   _preposition   object_

1. Below the cloudless sky the cattle grazed peacefully.

2. Many times during the battle the soldiers became weary.

3. After the rainstorm, a rainbow suddenly appeared.

4. She thought she had placed the receipt on the counter, but her husband found it on the floor.

5. Susie hid behind the door when the stranger entered.

6. Jasmine walked toward the gate in the flower garden.

7. Mother walked up the steps to the doctor's office.

8. Over the hill and down the valley we went.

9. Mrs. Starks said that we couldn't leave without them.

10. Our house is behind the school and beside the park.

11. Father said that we could stay until noon.

12. From Jay's house to mine, it is 12 miles.

13. Let's meet near the ice cream parlor on the corner.

© RBP Books

Practicing with Prepositions

Directions: In the following sentences, write three prepositions that could be used to complete the sentences.

Example: The girls walked **near** the horse stables.
The girls walked **beside** the horse stables.
The girls walked **through** the horse stables.

1. Dr. Harrison stood _____ the patient's bed.

2. What is _____ the television?

3. Jonathan and Arnold live _____ the football stadium.

4. Those oranges are _____ the grocery sack.

5. The cardinals flew _____ the birdhouse.

6. Place the flowers _____ the table _____ the bowl.

7. The magazine _____ the coffee table is Yegor's.

8. The silly girls talked _____ the movie.

9. The woman stood _____ the truck _____ the rosebush.

10. Please put the desserts _____ the dining room table.

www.summerbridgeactivities.com
©RBP Books

Reviewing Prepositions

Directions: In the following story, underline the prepositional phrases. Remember: Prepositional phrases begin with words such as *in*, *on*, *for*, *from*, *by*, *before*, and so forth. Circle the object of each prepositional phrase.

Most bats are devoted mates and will not separate from one another. When bats migrate, they climb to more than ten thousand feet to cruise. Of the 155 species of mammals in Belize, 85 of them are bats. Bats are the only true flying mammals and are champions of aeronautics.

Bats can hibernate at will. When a hibernating bat is disturbed, its body temperature rises to prepare for escape. If food is scarce, bats can hibernate until better times.

Where bats hang isn't random. Each bat has its own berth on the wall, and they roost near a cave entrance. They are loyal to the caves of their birth.

Bats use a sonar system. It is one thousand times more sophisticated than any of humankind's inventions. They use this sonar system to navigate as they are flying and to locate food.

A bat can scoop things up with its wing. It can cradle a baby in the bottom of its wing. A bat can also wrap a wing around itself like a shawl or use it to slingshot food into its mouth.

© RBP Books

Identifying Parts of Speech

In each sentence, identify the part of speech of the underlined word (noun, pronoun, adjective, adverb, or preposition) and write it in the blank provided.

Example: An adult <u>insect</u> has three body regions. <u>noun</u>

1. The head of an insect <u>contains</u> the eyes, the antennae, and the mouth parts. _____

2. The mouth parts <u>of</u> adult insects vary. _____

3. The head of most <u>adult</u> insects has a pair of antennae used to detect odors. _____

4. The thorax is the middle section of an adult <u>insect</u>. _____

5. Each segment <u>of</u> the thorax has one pair of legs. _____

6. Adult <u>insects</u> have six legs. _____

7. Most adult insects <u>usually</u> have two pairs of wings. _____

8. The wings of some insects are <u>leathery</u>. _____

9. The abdomen is the last section of the body, and <u>it</u> is composed of 11 segments. _____

10. Some insects' wings <u>have</u> hairs or scales. _____

11. An insect's <u>eyes</u> are often compound. _____

12. The <u>different</u> types of mouth parts determine how an insect will feed. _____

48

© RBP Books

Mixed-Up Parts of Speech

Directions: According to the following system, number each word in the groups of words; then copy the words in order.

1 = article, 2 = adjective, 3 = noun, 4 = verb, 5 = adverb

 **Example:**   3   4   2   1   5
apple fell red a down
A red apple fell down.

1. barked big dog loudly the

_____

2. continuously happy smiled woman a

_____

3. huge cautiously truck a drove

_____

4. high orange an bounced ball

_____

5. beautifully marvelous played orchestra the

_____

6. nearby clown funny performed a

_____

49

What Is a Sentence?

A **sentence** is a group of words that tells a complete thought. A sentence must tell who or what and what is or what happens.

Example: Fred ran home. (sentence)

Ran home quickly. (not a sentence)

Who or what?	**What is or what happens?**
Dr. Richardson	operated on the patient.
My old green car	is very dirty.

Directions: Identify which groups of words are sentences by writing the letter *S* in the blank. If the group of words does not form a sentence, write *NS*.

____ **1.** Mrs. Drake sang in the church choir.

____ **2.** The large cat purred as I petted her.

____ **3.** Marcia cried loudly.

____ **4.** Drove to the grocery store in the afternoon.

____ **5.** Kelly dug up the weeds in her garden.

____ **6.** Kenny replaced the countertops in the kitchen.

____ **7.** Cynthia, the manager, at the toy store.

____ **8.** The computer worked beautifully today.

____ **9.** Chased the squirrels up the large pine tree.

____ **10.** The experienced plumber in the dark hallway.

www.summerbridgeactivities.com

©RBP Books

Types of Sentences

There are four types of sentences. A sentence that tells something is a **statement**. A statement ends with a period (.). A sentence that asks something is a **question**. A question ends with a question mark (**?**). A sentence that tells someone to do something is a command. A **command** ends with a period (.).

A sentence that shows strong feeling, such as surprise, fear, or excitement, is an exclamation. An **exclamation** ends with an exclamation point (**!**).

 The cows grazed in the pasture. (statement)
What are you doing in there? (question)
Sit up straight in your chair. (command)
That car almost hit you! (exclamation)

Directions: In the following sentences, write *S* for statement, *Q* for question, *C* for command, or *E* for exclamation. Add the appropriate punctuation.

_____ **1.** Steve, where are you going

_____ **2.** Stand next to your desk

_____ **3.** Every day Nell jogs for five miles

_____ **4.** I can't wait to see Tom Cruise

_____ **5.** Did Ed tell you what is in the package

_____ **6.** My Aunt Peggy was a wonderful cook

_____ **7.** Open this jar of pickles

_____ **8.** That house is on fire

51

© RBP Books

Subjects and Predicates

All sentences have two parts, the **subject** and the **predicate**. The subject tells who or what the sentence is about. The predicate tells what the subject does or is. All words that tell who or what the sentence is about make up the **complete subject**. All words that tell something about the subject make up the **complete predicate**.

Complete Subject	Complete Predicate
Princess Diana	wore beautiful clothes.
The tall green plant	grew quite fast in the foyer.
Chicago	is known as "the windy city."

Directions: Draw a vertical line between the complete subject and the complete predicate.

1. Janet collected dolls from all over the world.

2. My younger brother Chuck has graduated from college.

3. The rabbi visited the elderly at the nursing home.

4. My sister Agatha washed all the dirty dishes in the sink.

5. Many interesting people attended church.

6. The boys and girls competed in the kite flying contest.

7. Everyone except Marcus approved the new officers.

8. Brazil is the largest country in South America.

9. The pope visited the Canadian province of Quebec.

10. It rained last Friday afternoon.

© RBP Books

Simple Subjects and Simple Predicates

The **simple subject**, which can be a noun or pronoun, is the main word that tells who or what the sentence is about. The **simple predicate**, which is always a verb, is the most important word in the complete predicate.

Directions: Underline the simple subject in the sentences.

Example: The brown <u>bears</u> were hibernating.

1. Yellowstone is the oldest national park in the world.

2. The park has more than 10,000 hot springs and geysers.

3. It is the home of grizzly bears and herds of bison.

4. Humans lived in this region for more than 12,000 years.

5. Hundreds of campers flock to Yellowstone National Park.

Directions: Underline the simple predicate in the sentences.

Example: Brown bears <u>were hibernating</u>.

6. Yellowstone is the oldest national park in the world.

7. The park has more than 10,000 hot springs and geysers.

8. It is the home of grizzly bears and herds of bison.

9. Humans lived in this region for more than 12,000 years.

10. Hundreds of campers flock to Yellowstone National Park.

© RBP Books Grammar Grade 4—RBP0113

Compound Subjects and Predicates

When a sentence has two or more subjects joined by *and* or *or*, the subject is called a **compound subject**. When a sentence has two or more predicates joined by *and* or *or*, the predicate is called a **compound predicate**.

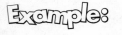 **Florida and California** are two of the leading tourist states. (compound subject)

Thousands of visitors **swim and play** in the warm ocean waters. (compound predicate)

Directions: Underline the compound predicates in the following sentences.

1. Daytona Beach, Fort Lauderdale, and Panama City are popular seaside resorts.

2. Florida's population and development are growing rapidly.

3. Sandy beaches, a sunny climate, and mineral sand deposits are some of Florida's natural resources.

4. Oranges, grapefruits, and tangerines are some of the main citrus fruits grown in Florida.

Directions: Underline the compound predicates in the following sentences.

5. Some tourists fly or drive to reach the Sunshine State.

6. Many residents in Florida farm, mine, or fish for a living.

7. Oranges, grapefruits, and tangerines are grown and processed in Florida.

8. Many hurricanes damage and destroy property in Florida.

 ©RBP Books

Combining Sentences: Compound Sentences

Sometimes the ideas in two short sentences are related in some way. If the ideas are related, you can combine the two short sentences to make one **compound sentence**. The two sentences can be joined by connecting words (conjunctions) like *and*, *or*, and *but*. A comma is generally used before the connecting word.

 Debbie rides her bike. Todd plays basketball.
Debbie rides her bike, **and** Todd plays basketball.

Richard plays the violin. Leo plays the guitar.
Richard plays the violin, **but** Leo plays the guitar.

Directions: Combine each pair of sentences into one compound sentence. Use the given connecting word.

1. Alice studies very hard. Jackie hates to study. (but)

_____

2. The Texas trip was long. The scenery was beautiful. (but)

_____

3. Carl read a book. Patrick played his video games. (and)

_____

4. You need to wash your clothes. There won't be any clean clothes. (or)

_____

5. We went to the zoo. We saw the giraffes. (and)

_____

© RBP Books

Correcting Run-On Sentences

When two sentences run into each other, they make a **run-on sentence**. Run-on sentences should not be used in your writing. A run-on sentence can be corrected by writing each complete thought as a separate sentence.

 My uncle teaches middle school he teaches geography. (incorrect)

My uncle teaches middle school. He teaches geography. (correct)

Directions: Correct the following run-on sentences by writing them as two complete sentences.

1. Jabria likes spaghetti she likes garlic bread.

_____

2. Some people enjoy basketball others enjoy soccer.

_____

3. Isabelle likes diet cola Coco likes regular cola.

_____

4. Daniela ran to school she walked to gymnastics.

_____

5. I walked to the park Valerie drove her car to the park.

_____

6. Two men sat at the barber shop they talked as they sat.

_____

7. It rained all night long it rained all day long.

_____

56

©RBP Books

Subject-Verb Agreement

The subject of a sentence must agree with its verb. If the subject is singular, use a singular form of the verb. If the subject is plural, use a plural form of the verb.

Singular Subject
When the subject is a singular noun or the pronoun *he*, *she*, or *it*, add *-s* to the verb.

Example: A doctor **helps** people. He **cures** aches.

Plural Subject
When the subject is a plural noun or the pronouns *I*, *we*, *you*, or *they*, do not add *-s* to the verb.

Example: Doctors **help** people. They **cure** aches.

Directions: Choose the verb that correctly completes each sentence.

1. Robert (want, wants) to be a doctor.

2. Danell (answer, answers) the switchboard at the office.

3. Many companies (buy, buys) their products on-line.

4. The Van Lohs (live, lives) in Sioux Falls, South Dakota.

5. Paul (know, knows) too much about writing books.

6. The men in our company (work, works) diligently.

7. My sister Jenica (like, likes) to paint landscape scenes.

8. Computers (help, helps) people in their everyday jobs.

9. The football coaches (require, requires) the players to run and practice every day.

10. I (wonder, wonders) how I ever did all that work.

© RBP Books

Subject-Verb Agreement

Subject-verb agreement often becomes confusing when using irregular verbs. Forms of the verb *to be* are especially confusing.

Singular Present/Past		**Plural** Present/Past	
I am	I was	we are	we were
you are	you were	you are	you were
he is	he was	they are	they were
she is	she was		
it is	it was		

Directions: Underline the verb that correctly completes the sentence.

1. I (am, are) going to the skating rink with my friend.

2. You (are, were) late for the surprise party.

3. She (is, was) sitting at home now feeling sorry for herself.

4. They (are, were) roller blading in Sunshine Park.

5. It (is, was) a beautiful day on Tuesday.

6. He (is, was) singing and dancing in the musical tonight.

7. You (are, were) the first one to finish your work yesterday.

8. She (is, was) learning how to bake a cake last night.

9. He (is, was) brushing his dog early this morning before he left.

58

©RBP Books

Capitalization

Use **capital letters** when writing the following things:

- the first word in a sentence
- proper nouns—names of particular people, places, or things
- the pronoun *I*
- important words in titles of stories, movies, books, and so forth

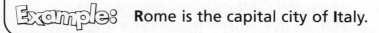 **Example:** Rome is the capital city of Italy.

Directions: Write each sentence correctly on the line.

1. one of the greatest scientists of all time was albert einstein.

_____

2. einstein was born on march 14, 1879, in germany.

_____

3. *albert einstein and the frontiers of physics* is a book written by jeremy bernstein.

_____

_____

4. in 1909 einstein became a professor at the university of zurich.

_____

5. he also became a professor at the german university in prague.

_____

6. in 1933, while visiting england and the united states, the german government took away his citizenship.

_____

_____

© RBP Books

Capitalization

Capitalize holidays, special events, days of the week, months of the year, geographical locations, and periods in history.

 holidays—Memorial **Day**
special events—Election **Day**
days of the week—**Thursday**
months of the year—**July**
geographical locations—**Mount Everest**
periods in history—the **Middle Ages**

Directions: In the following sentences, underline the word(s) that should be capitalized.

1. the lewis and clark expedition was an early exploration of what is now the northwestern united states.

2. they journeyed up the missouri river, across the rocky mountains, and along the columbia river.

3. the men began to plan an expedition to chart a route through the louisiana territory and the oregon region.

4. on may 14, 1804, the expedition began from camp dubois.

5. as lewis and clark traveled up the missouri river, they were amazed by the beauty of the land.

6. crossing the mountains in idaho was the most difficult part of the journey.

7. in november 1805, the explorers reached the pacific coast.

© RBP Books

Capitalization

Capitalize a **title** when it comes before a person's name. If the title is more than one word, capitalize every important word. Some titles may be written out or abbreviated. To show respect, some titles are capitalized when they are used in place of the person's name. Also, capitalize particular things, such as **nationalities** and **brand names**.

Example: titles—**P**resident Lincoln, **R**everend Clark
nationalities—**M**exican, **C**hinese
brand names—**C**oca-**C**ola, **P**epsi

Directions: Capitalize titles, nationalities, brand names, and any other appropriate words below.

1. mr. benjamin franklin

_____

2. german chocolate cake

_____

3. nike basketball shoes

_____

4. cocoa puffs

_____

5. the european woman

_____

6. vice president al gore

_____

7. dr. john harrison

_____

8. native american man

_____

9. italian leather coat

_____

10. mrs. rhonda starling

_____

11. burger king whopper

_____

12. gray dell computer

_____

13. the canadian geese

_____

14. green polo shirt

_____

© RBP Books

Capitalization

Words that show **family relationship** are capitalized when they come before a person's name. If a family-relationship word is used by itself in place of a person's name, it is also capitalized. If a family-relationship word is used after a possessive, it is not capitalized. Family-relationship words are not capitalized when they are used by themselves and not in place of a name.

Example: Uncle Charlie, **M**om, my aunt, dads

An **initial** used in the place of a name is capitalized and followed by a period.

Example: Charles **F.** Stanley

Directions: Using the previous capitalization rules as well as the rules listed above, capitalize the appropriate words in the following sentences.

1. my aunt and uncle recently purchased a new buick.

_____

2. p. t. barnum organized the circus known as the greatest show on earth.

_____

3. on friday, august 27, we will be traveling to disney world.

_____

4. dr. martin luther king, jr., was born in atlanta, georgia.

_____

5. on labor day we picnicked in yellowstone national park.

_____

6. i wanted to buy some levi jeans and reebok shoes.

_____

 ©RBP Books

Punctuation: End Marks

A **period** is used to end a statement.

Example: The dog lay sleeping on the carpet.

A **period** is also used to end a command.

Example: Please open this can of beans.

A **question mark** is used to end a question.

Example: Where are my house keys?

An **exclamation mark** is used to end an exclamation.

Example: Look how fast the roller coaster is going!

Directions: Place the correct mark at the end of each sentence.

1. Take the garbage can to the curb

2. What time is your bus arriving

3. My bus is scheduled to arrive at 8:10

4. Do you know who will be the bus driver today

5. I can't believe how bumpy this bus ride is

6. Look at that huge fish that jumped out of the lake

7. The fish was at least ten pounds

8. Are you wearing your life jacket

9. No, I am not wearing my life jacket

10. Put your life jacket on right now

11. Will you bait my hook

12. How many fish have you caught today

© RBP Books

Punctuation: Abbreviations and Initials

Some words have a shortened form called an **abbreviation**. Most abbreviations begin with a capital letter and end with a period. Some common abbreviations are

Titles	**Mr.**	mister	**Mrs.**	married woman
	Jr.	junior	**Ms.**	any woman
	Sr.	senior	**Dr.**	doctor
Addresses	**Rd.**	road	**Co.**	company
	St.	street	**P.O.**	post office
	Ave.	avenue	**Blvd.**	boulevard
Months	**Jan.**	January	**Sept.**	September
	Apr.	April	**Nov.**	November
Days	**Sun.**	Sunday	**Wed.**	Wednesday
	Tues.	Tuesday	**Thurs.**	Thursday
States*	**GA**	Georgia	**VT**	Vermont
	KS	Kansas	**OR**	Oregon

* Special two-letter abbreviations for state names are used with zip codes. Both letters are capitalized and no period is used.

Directions: Write the correct abbreviation for each underlined word.

1. <u>Doctor</u> John Spilane

_____

2. Monday, <u>December</u> 29

_____

3. 18 Sycamore <u>Street</u>

_____

4. Thomas Ashley McCoy, <u>Junior</u>

_____

5. Scott Biscuit <u>Company</u>

_____

6. 7552 Eastern <u>Avenue</u>

_____

7. <u>Mister</u> Paul Reed

_____

8. (<u>married woman</u>) Anna Sanchez

_____

©RBP Books

Punctuation: Dates, Greetings, Closings, Cities, and States

A **comma** (,) is placed between the date of the month and the year. A comma is also used after the year within a sentence.

Example: On April 19, 1976, Jerry Franks was born.

A **comma** (,) is placed after the greeting in a friendly letter and after the closing in any letter.

Example: Dear Aunt Martha,
Yours truly,

A **comma** (,) is placed between the name of a city and the state, district, or country.

Example: Paris, France Dallas, Texas

Directions: Using commas, correctly punctuate the following:

1. On January 3 1959 Alaska became a state.

2. Her pen pal lives in Olympia Washington.

3.   January 10 2003
Dear Mr. Walker
                               Sincerely
                               Jackie Griffith

4. George Starks is traveling to Bangkok Thailand.

5. Santa Fe New Mexico is a great place to live.

6. On May 14 2000 I went on a trip to Lima Peru.

7. George Strait is performing on June 23 2003.

8. Dear Mrs. Ellington
                               Sincerely yours

© RBP Books

Punctuation: Commas in a Series

Use **commas** to separate words in a series of three or more items. Use *and* before the last word in a series. Note: Do not place a comma after the last word in a series.

 Dogs, cats, **and** hamsters make good pets.

A red cup, a blue saucer, **and** a green plate were on the old, wooden picnic table.

Directions: Place commas where needed in the following sentences.

1. The huge old green house on Grant Avenue was vacant.

2. Jim Julie John and Jackie were all very good friends.

3. Mother cooked green beans potatoes carrots and roast beef for dinner.

4. For homework tonight I have English spelling math and social studies.

5. Greg ran jumped skated and fell down from exhaustion.

6. The clarinet trumpet saxophone and drums are my favorite musical instruments.

7. The high fluffy white clouds filled the blue summer sky.

8. On our vacation we visited Massachusetts Connecticut Vermont and New Hampshire.

www.summerbridgeactivities.com   ©RBP Books

Contractions

A **contraction** is one word made from two words. One form of contraction is made with a **verb + not**. Another form of contraction is made with a **pronoun + a verb**. An apostrophe is used to show where letters have been omitted.

Example:

is + not = **isn't**   are + not = **aren't**

do + not = **don't**   will + not = **won't**

had + not = **hadn't**   have + not = **haven't**

he + is = **he's**   you + will = **you'll**

Directions: Complete the missing words in the chart below.

Two Words	Contraction
1. there is	
2. will not	
3.	aren't
4. they had	
5. I had	
6.	you're
7. it is	
8.	I'm
9. do not	
10. they are	
11. she had	
12.	it'll
13. they have	
14. is not	
15.	she's
16. you will	
17. he is	
18. had not	
19. she would	
20.	we'd

© RBP Books

Troublesome Words: Homonyms

Words that are pronounced the same but have different spellings and different meanings are **homonyms**.

Example:

to, too, two	here, hear
their, there, they're	hour, our
by, bye, buy	for, four
week, weak	see, sea
knew, new	plane, plain
write, right	won, one
way, weigh	ate, eight

Directions: Underline the correct homonym in each sentence.

1. (There, Their, They're) will be basketball tryouts next (weak, week).

2. The teenager wanted to (by, bye, buy) some (knew, new) basketball shoes.

3. Each player had to (way, weigh) in before (there, their, they're) practice.

4. The next game will begin at (ate, eight) o'clock in the school gymnasium.

5. Our practices usually last (one, won) or (to, too, two) (ours, hours).

6. (Hour, Our) opponents arrived by (plain, plane) (for, four) hours before the game started.

7. Coach Jones commented that every play was performed exactly (write, right).

8. The first night we wore our (knew, new) uniforms, we (one, won) the game.

 © RBP Books

Troublesome Words: Antonyms and Synonyms

Words that have nearly the same meaning are called **synonyms**. Your writing will be more interesting if you do not use the same words over and over. Use your thesaurus to look up synonyms.

Example: small, little, tiny   big, large, huge

Antonyms are words that have opposite meanings. Use antonyms to show how places, things, or people are different. You can also find antonyms in your thesaurus.

Example: big, little   up, down

Directions: Replace each underlined word with a synonym. If necessary, use a thesaurus.

1. The <u>small</u> boy started to run in front of a large truck.

2. The <u>big</u> man jumped out of his truck and ran to the boy.

3. Johnny, the <u>little</u> boy, <u>started</u> crying when the man picked him up.

4. Johnny's mother was <u>glad</u> that he was not injured.

Directions: Choose the word in parentheses that is an antonym for the underlined word.

5. Beth was <u>happy</u> when she saw the movie. (glad, sad)

6. The movie was long and <u>interesting</u>. (boring, exciting)

7. Beth's friend, Katie, thought the movie was <u>entertaining</u>. (dull, amusing)

8. Their friends really <u>enjoyed</u> the movie too. (disliked, loved)

© RBP Books

Goofy Grammar

Directions: This is fun to do with friends; however, you can do this on your own, too. Before reading the story, fill in the blanks below with a word for each category. Then, using the words you have chosen, fill in the blanks in the story. Next, read the story aloud with your words. Have fun!

Story 1		Story 2	
common noun	_____	common noun	_____
adjective	_____	adjective	_____
verb	_____	adjective	_____
common noun (place)	_____	adjective	_____
verb	_____	common noun (place)	_____
collective noun	_____	common noun (place)	_____
adjective	_____	common noun	_____
collective noun	_____	verb	_____
adjective	_____	common noun	_____
common noun	_____	verb	_____
plural noun	_____	common noun	_____
adjective	_____	common noun	_____
common noun	_____	adjective	_____
subject pronoun	_____		
proper noun (name)	_____		
plural noun	_____		
adverb	_____		

70

© RBP Books

Goofy Grammar Story 1

Once upon a time there was a big, green,

fire-breathing _____. His name was Al.
      <u>common noun</u>

Now Al was very _____. All that Al did all day long was
           <u>adjective</u>

to _____ in his _____ and _____, that is,
   <u>verb</u>   <u>common noun (place)</u>   <u>verb</u>

except for his occasional trips into the _____ to find food.
                                    <u>collective noun</u>

When Al _____ into the forest, he would see birds
        <u>adjective</u>

flying in their _____ and families of rabbits hopping
              <u>collective noun</u>

along together. This just made him _____. Al longed for
                                 <u>adjective</u>

family and _____. This was a problem because of his fire
          <u>common noun</u>

breathing. Most _____ wanted nothing to do with Al.
               <u>plural noun</u>

That is until one day when a large, _____, fire-breath-
                                  <u>adjective</u>

ing, _____ came along. _____ name was
    <u>common noun</u>   <u>subject pronoun</u>

_____. They both knew that they were going to be good
<u>proper noun (name)</u>

_____. They also knew that they were meant to be
<u>plural noun</u>

friends forever. They have lived _____ ever since.
                               <u>adverb</u>

71

Goofy Grammar Story 2

The hippopotamus is also known as the

"river _____." Their bodies are barrel
common noun

shaped and _____. They have a/an _____ belly, a
adjective adjective

large head, and _____ legs. They live in _____,
adjective common noun (place)

_____, and swamps.
common noun (place)

The hippo is a relative of camels, pigs, and _____.
common noun

Most of the hippo's day is spent _____ in the _____.
verb common noun

Sometimes hundreds of hippos share a territory of water

during the day. Hippos will play, mate, fight, give birth, and

_____ in the water.
verb

A few hours after sunset, the hippos leave the water to graze

on _____ by the light of the _____. So many
common noun common noun

hippos use the same path out of the water at dusk that it

becomes _____ Often it is worn five or six feet deep.
adjective

Other animals also use these paths to get to the water.

 ©RBP Books

Answer Pages

Page 1
1. San Francisco, coast, California, peninsula, landfall, Golden Gate
2. channel, Golden Gate Bridge, symbol, city, port, entry, Pacific coast
3. city, attraction, views, hills
4. lines, landmarks, hills
5. Nob Hill, Chinatown, communities, Asia, Telegraph Hill, location, station
6. Fisherman's Wharf, port, immigrants, row, restaurants, shops, hotels
7. San Francisco Bay, prison, Alcatraz, structure, currents, waters

Page 2
1. P = Lucy, Oak Tree Park
   C = father, kitten
2. P = Marie, Miss Muffet
   C = sister, kitten, rhyme
3. P = Jonathan, Pet Town, Miss Muffet
   C = brother, food, bowl, bed
4. P = Pet Town, Lucy, Mrs. York, Duke
   C = teacher, treats, dog
5. P = Lucy, Mrs. Johnson, Miss Muffet
   C = home, mother, leg
6. P = Lucy, Miss Muffet
   C = mother, damage, kitten
7. P = Miss Muffet, Johnson family
   C = hours, enjoyment, entertainment family
8. P = Miss Muffet; C = family

Page 3
1. gifts	2. prizes	3. puddles
4. stores	5. students	6. cafeterias
7. houses	8. chairs	9. mouths
10. papers	11. drums	12. floors
13. curtains	14. desks	15. bands
16. seas	17. flags	18. birds
19. turkeys	20. keys	21. ducks
22. boats	23. costumes	24. elephants
25. teachers	26. biscuits	27. hamsters
28. necklaces		

Page 4
1. boxes, 4	2. coaches, 4	3. sheep, 8
4. patches, 4	5. brushes, 4	6. geese, 7
7. donkeys, 3	8. shelves, 6	9. classes, 4
10. knives, 6	11. mice, 7	12. berries, 2

Page 5
1. Melissa, PR; Andrew, PR; boy, C; Chandler, PR
2. Chandler, PR; formula, C; noises, C, PL
3. McCoys, PR, PL; Chandler, PR; Christmas, PR; aunts, C, PL; uncles, C, PL; cousins, C, PL; baby, C
4. boys, C, PL; family, C; girls, C, PL; men, C, PL; family, C
5. Melissa, PR; sisters, C, PL; Andrea, PR; Erin, PR; brother, C; Matthew, PR; Andrew, PR; brothers, C, PL; Jonathan, PR; Richard, PR
6. Chandler, PR; grandchild, C; families, C, PL; presents, C, PL; members, C, PL
7. Nana, PR; Papa, PR; grandparents, C, PL; pictures, C, PL

Page 6
1. flock	2. class	3. committee
4. fleet	5. litter	6. orchestra
7. team	8. jury	9. club
10. crowd		

Page 7
A <u>cheetah</u> is elegant and graceful. Running at <u>speeds</u> of up to 70 <u>miles</u> per hour, the <u>cheetah</u> is by far the fastest of the <u>cat family</u>(CN). <u>Cheetahs</u> were once found in most of <u>Africa</u>, the <u>Middle East</u>, and <u>India</u>. Now they are found mostly in sub-Saharan <u>Africa</u>. The <u>cheetah</u> has long, muscular <u>legs</u>; a small, round <u>head</u>; a long <u>neck</u>; and special <u>pads</u> on its <u>feet</u> for <u>traction</u>. Even though the <u>cheetah</u> is fast, it cannot speed for long <u>distance</u> because it may overheat.

When a <u>cheetah</u> makes a <u>kill</u>, it eats quickly and keeps an <u>eye</u> out for <u>scavengers</u>, such as <u>leopards</u> and <u>vultures</u>. They usually hunt smaller <u>antelopes</u> and <u>impalas</u>.

If hunting together, they may seek out a <u>herd</u>(CN) of <u>zebras</u> or <u>wildebeests</u>. Even though the <u>cheetah</u> is fast, it depends on <u>cover</u> to hide in as it stalks its <u>prey</u>(CN). The <u>cheetah</u> gets as close as possible to its <u>prey</u>(CN) and then uses a <u>burst</u> of <u>speed</u> to outrun its <u>quarry</u>(CN).

Page 8
1. I	2. we, we	3. she, them
4. I, her, me	5. it	6. they, we, it
7. it, us, them	8. she, I	

© RBP Books Grammar Grade 4—RBP0113

Answer Pages

Page 9
1. she, her   2. him, he   3. them, they
4. her, it   5. it   6. she, her
7. they, them   8. it   9. she, he, her
10. they, them   11. He   12. it
13. they   14. They   15. She
16. You   17. We   18. He

Page 10
1. He/She   2. They   3. it   4. She
5. he   6. It   7. They

Page 11
1. them   2. me   3. us   4. him   5. it
6. you   7. her   8. us   9. them

Page 12
1. I, subject   2. me, object   3. We, subject
4. her, object   5. they, subject   6. His, subject
7. we, subject   8. it, object

Page 13
Our, his, their, My, our, its, his, their

Page 14
1. hers   2. yours   3. mine   4. his
5. theirs   6. ours   7. mine   8. theirs
9. his   10. ours   11. his   12. yours

Page 15
1. they'll   2. you've   3. I'll

Page 16
1. I am   2. You are   3. They are
4. You had   5. I have   6. he is
7. It is   8. We would   9. he has
10. We are

Page 17
1. his   2. They   3. She   4. they
5. Her   6. his,   7. its
8. Their   9–11. Answers will vary.
12. they are   13. she would or she had
14. you shall or you will

Page 18
1. form, meet   2. reach   3. live, go
4. cause   5. break, damage
6. Protect   7. form   8. move
9. lie   10. announced
11. indicates

Page 19
1. is   2. were   3. are   4. were   5. am
6. was   7. were   8. are   9. is

Page 20
1. walks, rides, talks
2. walked, rode, talked
3. will walk, will ride, will talk
4. will go   5. gather or gathered
6. walked   7. will operate
8. used   9. build

Page 21
1. future   2. past   3. present   4. past
5. future   6. past   7. past
8. past, present   9. present

Page 22 Answers may vary.
1. did   2. was   3. is   4. am
5. will, may, should, or could
6. would   7. must   8. can   9. were

Page 23
1. has learned   2. Have gone swim
3. are practicing   4. will be held
5. was driving   6. Did go
7. am competing   8. is swimming
9. should win   10. was excited

Page 24
1. did   2. ran   3. took   4. went
5. slept   6. began   7. worn   8. flew
9. won   10. sold

Page 25
1. causes 2. form   3. strikes   4. creates
5. cheer   6. cries   7. occur   8. happen
9. ruin

Page 26
move, walk, ruin, sang, run, shall, swimming, rides, learned, flying, practice, coach, indicate, went, visit, cry, protect, fly, were, strike, are, sold, am, cause, take.
1–6. Answers may vary.

Page 27
1. A. noun, B. verb   2. A. verb, B. noun
3. A. verb, B. noun   4. A. verb, B. noun
5. A. noun, B. verb   6. A. noun, B. verb

www.summerbridgeactivities.com   © RBP Books

Answer Pages

Page 28

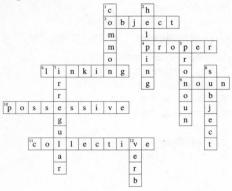

Crossword answers:
- 3. object
- 4. proper
- 6. linking
- 9. noun
- 10. possessive
- 11. collective

Page 29

1. largest, what kind
2. Many, how many
3. Those, which ones; corn, what kind; delicious, what kind
4. One, how many; popular, what kind
5. nine, how many
6. These, which one; nine, how many
7. highest, what kind
8. ancient, what kind; Aztec, what kind
9. those, which ones; beautiful, what kind; Mexican, what kind

Page 30 (Possible answers)

The African parrot lives in tropical areas. One variety is **the** rose-ringed parakeet. It has **a** long tail, **a** bright red bill, and **a** bright green head. **The** nine species of lovebirds are **the** only small African parrots. **The** lovebirds have short, rounded tails and rather large bills. **The** lovebirds got their name because they were thought to mate for life. **A/The** large, grey parrot from **the/a** west African rain forest is **a** popular pet bird because it can learn to say words.

Page 31

1. The largest
2. Some, the
3. one, the fastest
4. brown, green, some, black
5. A, few, bright, green, orange, red, yellow
6. The, most, hard
7. Land, heavy, short, club-like
8. Most, freshwater, the, warm, muddy, a, other

Page 32

1. angry
2. happy, excited
3. kind
4. powerful, overwhelming
5. colorful, talented, entertaining
6. tall, funny
7. loud, fierce, scary
8. graceful, daring
9. lively, hilarious

Page 33

1. older, oldest
2. clearer, clearest
3. taller, tallest
4. quicker, quickest
5. faster, fastest
6. stronger, strongest
7. drier, driest
8. thinner, thinnest
9. redder, reddest
10. longer, longest
11. happier, happiest
12. cuter, cutest
13. tinier, tiniest
14. louder, loudest
15. angrier, angriest

Page 34

1. biggest
2. busiest
3. older
4. most historic
5. longest
6. largest
7. farther
8. most fashionable

Page 35

1. best
2. worst
3. better
4. better
5. worse
6. better

Page 36

1. A 2. B 3. B 4. A 5. B 6. B 7. A 8. B 9. A

Page 37

1. fairly
2. Once
3. Now, quickly
4. thoughtfully
5. formally
6. gracefully
7. Surprisingly
8. only
9. most

Page 38

1. early→arrived
2. already→left
3. forlornly→watched
4. carefully→packed
5. backwards→walking
6. Fortunately→were broken
7. difficulty→loading
8. quickly →loaded
9. Soon→say
10. Completely→packed, early→left

Page 39

(Answers may vary.) Suggested answers: extremely, suddenly, quickly, happily, quickly, Soon, Next, thoroughly, completely, soon, smoothly, enthusiastically, certainly

© RBP Books

Answer Pages

Page 40
1. faster, fastest
2. more gracefully, most gracefully
3. higher, highest
4. more loudly, most loudly

Page 41
1. well   2. surely   3. really   4. well
5. badly   6. badly   7. really
8. surely   9. well   10. Surely

Page 42
1. ever   2. anywhere   3. no one
4. never   5. nothing   6. nobody
7. anyone   8. any

Page 43
1. very, beautifully
2. quickly, quietly
3. carefully, accurately
4. faster
5. politely   6. faster
7. extremely, very   8. recently
9. more skillfully   10. today
11. worse   12. faster
13. loudly   14. surely
15. well   16. most badly
17. unexpectedly   18. clumsily
19. steadily   20. everywhere
21–25. Answers will vary.

Page 44
1. over the rolling hills
2. of pine straw and twigs, in the trees
3. above the white fence
4. around the corner, of the street
5. on the porch steps
6. between Travis and me
7. except Harry, in this morning's race

Page 45
(Arrow points to object of the preposition.)
1. Below→sky
2. during→battle
3. After→rainstorm
4. on→counter, on→floor
5. behind→door
6. toward→gate, in→garden
7. up→steps, to→office
8. Over→hill, down→valley
9. without→them

10. behind→school, beside→park
11. until→noon
12. From→house, to→mine
13. near→ice cream parlor, on→corner

Page 46 (Answers may vary.)
1. beside, near, at
2. on, beside, beneath
3. around, behind, near
4. in, beside, beneath
5. to, under, from
6. near, beside, on; in, by, beside
7. on, near, beside
8. in, during, through
9. on, near, beside; near, beside, behind
10. on, by, near

Page 47
paragraph 1
    from one→another; to more than ten
    thousand→feet;
    Of the 155→species; of→mammals;
    in→Belize;
    of→them;
    of→aeronautics
paragraph 2
    at→will;
    for→ escape;
    until better→times
paragraph 3
    on the→wall, near a cave→entrance;
    to the → cave, of their→birth
paragraph 4
    of humankind's→inventions;
    with its→wing
paragraph 5
    in the→bottom; of its→wing;
    around→itself; into its→mouth

Page 48
1. verb   2. preposition   3. adjective
4. noun   5. preposition   6. noun
7. adverb   8. adjective   9. pronoun
10. verb   11. noun   12. adjective

www.summerbridgeactivities.com   ©RBP Books

Answer Pages

Page 49
1. The big dog barked loudly.
2. A happy woman smiled continuously.
3. A huge truck drove cautiously.
4. An orange ball bounced high.
5. The marvelous orchestra played beautifully.
6. A funny clown performed nearby.

Page 50
1. S   2. S   3. S   4. NS   5. S
6. S   7. NS   8. S   9. NS   10. NS

Page 51
1. Q (?)   2. C (.)   3. S (.)   4. E (!)
5. Q (?)   6. S (.)   7. C (.)   8. E (!)

Page 52
1. Janet I collected
2. Chuck I has graduated
3. rabbi I visited
4. Agatha I washed
5. people I attended
6. girls I competed
7. Marcus I approved
8. Brazil I is
9. pope I visited
10. It I rained

Page 53
1. Yellowstone   2. park
3. It   4. Humans
5. campers   6. is
7. has   8. is
9. lived   10. flock

Page 54
1. Daytona Beach, Fort Lauderdale, Panama City
2. population, development
3. beaches, climate, deposits
4. Oranges, grapefruits, tangerines
5. fly, drive
6. farm, mine, fish
7. grown, processed
8. damage, destroy

Page 55
1. Alice studies very hard, but Jackie hates to study.
2. The Texas trip was long, but the scenery was beautiful.
3. Carl read a book, and Patrick played his video games.
4. You need to wash your clothes, or there won't be any clean clothes.
5. We went to the zoo, and we saw the giraffes.

Page 56
1. Jabria likes spaghetti. She likes garlic bread.
2. Some people enjoy basketball. Others enjoy soccer.
3. Isabelle likes diet cola. Coco likes regular cola.
4. Daniela ran to school. She walked to gymnastics.
5. I walked to the park. Valerie drove her car to the park.
6. Two men sat at the barber shop. They talked as they sat.
7. It rained all night long. It rained all day long.

Page 57
1. wants   2. answers   3. buy   4. live
5. knows   6. work   7. likes
8. help   9. require   10. wonder

Page 58
1. am   2. were or are   3. is
4. are or were   5. was   6. is
7. were   8. was   9. was

Page 59
1. One of the greatest scientists of all time was Albert Einstein.
2. Einstein was born on March 14, 1879, in Germany.
3. *Albert Einstein and the Frontiers of Physics* is a book written by Jeremy Bernstein.
4. In 1909, Einstein became a professor at the University of Zurich.
5. He also became a professor at the German University in Prague.
6. In 1933, while visiting England and the United States, the German government took away his citizenship.

77

Answer Pages

Page 60
1. The Lewis, Clark Expedition, United States.
2. They, Missouri River, Rocky Mountains, Columbia River.
3. The, Louisiana Territory, Oregon.
4. On, May, Camp Dubois.
5. As, Lewis, Clark, Missouri River.
6. Crossing, Idaho.
7. In, November, Pacific.

Page 61
1. Mr. Benjamin Franklin   2. German
3. Nike   4. Cocoa Puffs   5. European
6. Vice President Al Gore
7. Dr. John Harrison
8. Native American   9. Italian
10. Mrs. Rhonda Starling
11. Burger King Whopper
12. Dell   13. Canadian   14. Polo

Page 62
1. My, Buick
2. P. T. Barnum, Greatest Show, Earth
3. On, Friday, August, Disney World
4. Dr. Martin Luther King, Jr., Atlanta, Georgia
5. On, Labor Day, Yellowstone National Park
6. I, Levi, Reebok

Page 63
1. (.)   2. (?)   3. (.)   4. (?)   5. (!)
6. (!)   7. (. or !) 8. (?)   9. (.)   10. (.)
11. (?)   12. (?)

Page 64
1. Dr.   2. Dec.   3. St.   4. Jr.
5. Co.   6. Ave.   7. Mr.   8. Mrs.

Page 65
1. January 3, 1959,
2. Olympia, Washington
3. January 10, Mr. Walker, Sincerely,
4. Bangkok, Thailand
5. Sante Fe, New Mexico,
6. May 14, 2000, Lima, Peru
7. June 23, 2003
8. Mrs. Ellington, Sincerely yours,

Page 66
1. The huge, old, green house on Grant Avenue was vacant.
2. Jim, Julie, John, and Jackie were all good friends.
3. Mother cooked green beans, potatoes, carrots, and roast beef for dinner.
4. For homework tonight I have English, spelling, math, and social studies.
5. Greg ran, jumped, skated, and fell down from exhaustion.
6. The clarinet, trumpet, saxophone, and drums are my favorite musical instruments.
7. The high, fluffy, white clouds filled the blue summer sky.
8. On our vacation we visited Massachusetts, Connecticut, Vermont, and New Hampshire.

Page 67
1. there's   2. won't   3. are not
4. they'd   5. I'd   6. you are
7. it's   8. I am   9. don't
10. they're   11. she'd   12. it will
13. they've   14. isn't   15. she is
16. you'll   17. he's   18. hadn't
19. she'd   20. we would or we had

Page 68
1. There, week   2. buy, new
3. weigh, their   4. eight
5. one, two, hours   6. Our, plane, four
7. right   8. new, won

Page 69 (Answers may vary.)
1. little   2. large
3. small, began   4. happy
5. sad   6. boring
7. dull   8. disliked

www.summerbridgeactivities.com   © RBP Books